HOW TO SAVE MONEY AND STILL HAVE FUN

Ambreen Hameed

TABLE OF CONTENT

INTRODUCTION

Who says I have to save... and how can it be fun???

Saving money-- sometimes nothing seems as if it could be more boring, right? For many of us, thinking about saving and finances is reminiscent of musty boardrooms and grumpy old men. Saving money also feels like something that strains us or even deprives us of the things we want in life.

The truth is that saving money can actually be enjoyable and, in the long term, bring new security to your life that allows you to enjoy the finer things. By changing your approach to your finances, you can have a transformative experience that teaches you to find new joy and life in what had seemed like a dry, boring experience in the past.

In this book, we will review the tips and tricks that make saving fun. We will also go through the basics of household finances, investing, credit, and more. The best way to start enjoying anything is to understand it thoroughly so that there are no unpleasant surprises! In this book, you'll learn how to save your coins, but you will also learn how to enjoy the process. As with anything, you need to learn the rules first *then* learn how to improvise. So we'll start out going through the basics of saving and achieving financial well-being, then we'll segue into the little tips and tricks that make saving fun for you and not a strain.

Why Save?

Whether you are just starting out in your first job or established in a 20-year career, saving money is crucial. Many of us think there will always be a time somewhere down the road to save. There won't be, not necessarily! You cannot let your financial well-being depend on hypotheticals.

The good news is, however, that it doesn't have to be a dry or boring process, but one that engages you and brings fulfillment to your life. With the advent of apps and mobile devices, saving is something you can enjoy and do and the go, as well.

There are any number of reasons why you should save. For one, you never know when you may need extra funds. Anything from a flat tire to an unexpected storm that dings your house can leave you with an unexpected payment in the thousands. Saving money for the proverbial rainy day is the main reason many save.

There is also retirement to think about, of course. For many of us, that seems far away. "I'll have time," we tell ourselves. Having enough for retirement takes time for the average person, since our salaries are not necessarily in the millions, right? Starting to save from your very first paycheck is the best way to ensure that you have a cushion later in life.

You may have children, as well. Have you considered how you will pay for college or for their weddings? These events can rack up bills in the tens of thousands and even, on occasion, the hundreds of thousands. While a hardworking student might get a scholarship to a university, you still want to make sure you have enough saved for the extras, including housing, food, books, etc.

Finally, there is the fact that having something in savings makes you look good to creditors. If you are applying for a new credit card or even a mortgage on a new home, having something in savings shows that you are to be trusted by a lender. We will go into mortgages a bit more later on, but suffice to say for now that having a few coins in the bank can only improve your chances when it comes to loans and credit!

So let's get started. Don't worry. It won't be torture! In fact, at the end of it, you will feel better about yourself and your future and more confident in what you can achieve for yourself and your family.

CHAPTER ONE

Savings Basics: Getting Started the Right Way!

The best place to start with savings is to discuss two things-- how much to save and how often. There is only one rule you need to adhere to when it comes to these things, as well:

Rule #1 - Be Consistent!

So how much should you save and how often should you save it? There's a simple answer to this, too:

10 percent 100 percent of the time!

You may have had a parent, grandparent, or advisor say this to you at some point-- "Put 10 percent of your paycheck into savings!" This is just good advice, and you need to do it. Every time, every paycheck.

Let's say that again-- every paycheck!

The catch is there is no fixed answer to the amount. That depends on you and your household needs. The 10 percent is flexible, but the 100 percent is not. Whatever you decide to save, it needs to happen every paycheck.

There is science behind this. A few years back, the UK explored some ideas around pension savings. Many experts thought that the best bet would be to require people to put money into their savings. What they found was that once it was automatic and once people believed that the money was essentially "gone." these individuals were able to save and didn't feel the pinch of "losing" that income.

So, let's get into the "how much." Whatever the amount, again, consistency is what matters! So make it a matter of protocol that you will save the same amount every paycheck.

How Much Should I Save?

Determining how much to save can be intimidating when you have to set yourself to making that exact deposit each and every paycheck. After all, bills and even income can fluctuate. The good news is that the amount you save depends on you and your needs... so there's some stress off your back for you!

Many financial experts recommend going as high as 20 percent off of each paycheck. A popular idea promoted by institutions such as TIAA encourages people to follow a 50/30/20 system: that is, putting 50 percent of income towards necessary items such as rent and utilities, 30 percent towards discretionary items such as clothing or dining, and then 20 percent into saving.

The truth is, that amount may be too much of a pinch for most of us. When you are living paycheck-to-paycheck or making a lower income or paying high rent, even 10 percent can put a strain on your household.

As stated, you can lower the percentage based on your budgetary needs; but whatever number you choose, make sure you stick with it and do it every paycheck! Consistency is what matters. (We will get into more detail in the next chapter about how you can calculate the amount you need, FYI.)

In the next chapter when we go through your household budget, you can then determine exactly how much to save. For now, let's look at a little trick that helps make saving money that much easier!

Automatic Deposits

Automatic deposits are a blessing to anyone having to save. They make your savings deposit each month, well, *automatic*, but the takeaway from that is that *you don't need to think about it.* Here's the little trick of the trade that makes automatic deposits so important-- it makes it as if the money wasn't even there in the first place. And if the money isn't there, you won't miss it.

You don't want to determine your savings deposit after everything else has been accounted for in your monthly budget. If you take this approach, you may end up rationalizing your way out of making the deposit! You want the amount set, and you want it to be a fixed part of your monthly budget. "Oh, I can save more next month" or "Retirement is so far away... what is 100 bucks now?" Don't let this thinking stop you from saving.

Automating your savings deposits stops this kind of behavior in its track. To save you from yourself, have your monthly savings deposited automatically without question and consider it a necessary household bill as you might the utilities or your rent payment.

Chances are your bank has an app and online banking tools that you can use to set up your automatic deposits. Schedule them for a time of the month when you have a bit more wiggle room; say, after the paycheck on the 15th, if most of your first paycheck of the month goes to rent or your mortgage payment. To be clear, you would still be adhering to the 10 percent (or whatever percent works for you), but you could deposit both amounts on the paycheck that gives you a bit more breathing room.

The main focus should be on ensuring that it actually happens every month.

Setting Realistic Savings Goals

The vast majority of financial experts say that you should save as much as you would need for 6 months of your usual expenses. In other words, if your expenses are 2500 a month, you want to have 15,000 in savings at all times. Of course, saving this much is not always an option for the average person or family. After all, surprise expenses can pop up, including medical bills or something as simple as a car repair. A bare minimum you should shoot for is having 3 months' worth of expenses in the bank.

Optimizing Your Debt to Income Ratio
As you proceed in your savings plan, an important component of this is also making a plan to drive down your debt and optimize your DTI ratio, also known as your Debt to Income Ratio. Your DTI ratio is a good indicator of your financial health and is also a key factor when companies consider you for home loans and credit.

There are actually two DTI ratios you need to consider: your back-end DTI ratio and your front-end DTI ratio. Your front-end DTI ratio indicates how much of your income goes to housing expenses. You calculate this figure with this formula:

Housing expenses / gross income = front-end DTI ratio

As an example, if your housing expenses, including your rent and renter's insurance is 1500 and your gross income is 3000, your DTI ratio would be:

1500 / 3000 = 0.5

Your back-end DTI ratio factors in different expenses. It takes into consideration what you spend on debt each month. This includes items such as credit card payments, loan payments, and student loan payments. You calculate your back-end DTI in this way:

Total loan payments / gross income = backend DTI ratio

So if your debt payments are $2150 and your gross income is $5000, the calculation would look like this:

2150 / 5000 = 0.43

Generally speaking, most mortgage companies will want your back-end DTI to be lower than 0.40. That is to say, your debt payments

should be less than 40 percent of your gross income. As you begin to save, consider trying to pay down your debts and improve these numbers. This can only help you in the long run. Once you have your savings in place and are ready to make a big purchase such as a car or a home, your financial health will be optimal, and you will look that much better to lenders.

CHAPTER TWO

Creating Your Household Budget

In order to determine how much to put into savings each paycheck, you need to put together a household budget. Your household budget will define how you spend every penny in your wallet or bank account. There will be discretionary funds for having a good time, don't worry! However, that will all be carefully accounted for.

In order to improvise in jazz, you have to learn the form first, right? Structure gives you the wiggle room you need to have fun with your money. By carefully budgeting your household funds you can have the confidence you need to enjoy your money and know exactly how much you can spend on the things you enjoy... while still saving!

Step One - Determine Your Income

For some of us, this is easy. We get one paycheck on a regular basis and know exactly what number to plug in for our income. For others, such as people who make freelance income, this number can be variable. The best bet for freelancers is to gauge income on contracts that have already been signed and jobs that have already been given the green light. You do not want to build a household budget around maybes! The upside of this approach is that you get some extra money each month when you book more jobs than your planned income for that month!

Also, remember that income includes items such as alimony or child support that you may receive. Make sure to include these in your income totals. Any amount that comes in as income needs to be monies that you can rely on consistently. A budget will not do its job if the income listed in it is unreliable and inconsistent!

Step Two - List your Static Expenses

Static expenses are the ones that don't change each month. Your rent is a good example or your car payment. Other bills such as a power or water bill might fluctuate, but your static bills won't. List them and double check their amounts, then total them.

Step Three - List your Non-Static Expenses

Next, you will want to make a list of any bills that fluctuate from month to month, such as a power bill or a cell phone bill. Here's an important trick-- use the largest total you have ever received for one of these bills as your guidepost, *not* the lowest bill. You want to budget for worst case scenarios, not easy months! Groceries falls under this category as well. Budgeting for groceries can be difficult-- appetites fluctuate, and the price of food fluctuates, too!

In 2013, the US Department of Agriculture estimated that a family of four needs to spend somewhere between $150 and 300 a week to eat a healthy, well-rounded diet.[1] Look at your usual costs by reviewing your bank or credit card statements and settle on a number that works for your family.

Step Four - Set a Budget for Miscellaneous Expenses

You need spending cash each month for smaller, miscellaneous purchases. These can be a lunch out with the family or a trip to the movies. Budget a reasonable amount for these events, not to exceed 30 percent of your overall income.

You also need to account for miscellaneous items you might need *but not expect* throughout the month. Perhaps a child in your daughter's class has a birthday party, and you need a gift or maybe a special holiday is coming up. Oftentimes, people forget to budget for these "unexpected" costs. Try to keep a set amount aside each month for these small purchases. It can be as small as $50; the good news is that if you don't spend it, you can put it right into your savings!

Step Five - Add Up Your Expenses and Calculate Your Net for the Month

Finally, take all of your expenses, add them together, and subtract them from your income. This will be your net for the month, or the amount you *clear* each month after paying your bills.

---

https://www.usatoday.com/story/news/nation/2013/05/01/grocery-costs-for-family/2104165/

Step Six - Determine your Savings Deposit Amount

After you have your net income for the month, you will want to determine the amount you will be putting into savings each month. As discussed, ideally this would be around 20 percent of your income! If that is not possible, set the bar lower... but keep to that bar every month! You will do this by plugging the amount you settle on back into your budget as a Static Expense, and you will set up automatic deposits as well. This way it is an assumed and automatic expense, and not something you can touch!

Common Mistakes with Budgets

In the next chapter, we will discuss some of the best methods for tracking and optimizing your budget. Whichever approach you take, keep in mind that the most important part is making it as pain-free for you as possible. Use the approach that works best for your needs and works best with the way your brain works. This makes the "hard" work of budgeting that much easier for you. Before we move on, though, let's take a look at some common budgeting mistakes that you want to avoid to make it as fun an experience as possible-- other than not budgeting at all, of course!

Confusing Luxury with Necessity

A new pair of shoes or fancy rims for your car are not necessities! Too many of us are not clear with ourselves about what we really need. Make sure that you are honest about what an actual necessity within your budget is and what is there for a bit of fun!

Too Much Deprivation

Didn't we just tell you that you need to know the difference between luxury and necessity? Well, that's so you know just how much fun you can have, not so you can have no fun at all! Always budget a bit of money for fun and splurging.

Not Involving the Family

If you have a partner, kids, or even a roommate, many a budget has been ruined by a lack of clarity with the rest of the people in the house. Make sure everyone is on board with your budget and understands the goal of your budget and savings.

Forcing Yourself into Tight Weeks

Just because the rent is due on the 1st doesn't mean you need to spend the next two weeks with $5 in the bank. With big bills that are budget busters, split them across paychecks, putting a bit aside from each check. This way you don't have to take a big hit on one paycheck alone!

CHAPTER THREE

Your Budget Method - What Makes it Fun for You?

Now comes the fun part. Every month you can have a bit of fun figuring out where the wiggle room is in your budget. It becomes like a game, even a fun competition with yourself! Where can you trim expenses? Do you really need those cookies on every grocery trip? Maybe just two trips to the movies instead of three this month? Set yourself challenges and see if you can't throw a little extra into savings each month.

In order to do this, you need to find the budgeting method that works best for you. What does this mean? Everyone is different, even when it comes to money. For some of us, engaging with an app might be the most entertaining (and responsible!) way to budget. For others, old-fashioned methods such as Excel spreadsheets or keeping cash in an envelope might be the better option. The best choice is always what works for you-- not what works for just anyone!

Online Budget Trackers

There are a number of ways you can track and monitor your budget. Personally, I prefer using a spreadsheet to create and monitor my household's monthly budget. This has the advantage of letting me see all the bills at once and also see in an instant how small tweaks to the budget will affect the next month or even months to come. For example, if a tax refund comes in, I can divide it into credit card payments, savings, and discretionary items in a few clicks and see how that affects the next month in the same instant.

There is also a wide range of online budget trackers you can use to plan out your budget. These options can be highly useful because they can more often than not import your account information from your bank, your credit card companies, and more. You can see everything in one place and even take advantage of graphs and pie charts to gauge your progress and performance over time. Some online budget trackers can also help you develop plans and stick with them, whether you want to increase savings or pay down credit cards.

Online budget trackers also make tracking finances and saving more fun! They are designed to engage and offer fun little add-ons like goal setting that help you visualize your happy financial future. Take a tour of some of the best options out there such as NerdWallet or Mint or even explore options offered by your household bank. These tools can make financial management fun and entertaining.

Using Cash for Spending

When it comes to your non-static costs that fluctuate each month, switching to cash spending can be a helpful way to monitor and control spending. Remember, your non-static costs include groceries and miscellaneous entertainment expenses such as going out to eat or going to the movies. Instead of using your debit card to spend the 'cash' needed for these expenses, take out your budgeted amount in cash and carry it with you throughout the month. In this way, you can see just how quickly the money flows out and stay within your budget!

Excel Spreadsheets or Handwritten Ledgers

Look, some of us still like to keep things old school. Plus, not all of us are all that comfortable with technology or apps. As a result, for many of us the better option is to track a budget using more straightforward methods. Personally, I prefer tracking my budget in an Excel spreadsheet that I designed myself. The advantage of this is that you can customize it to suit your needs to a tee. While budget trackers may have bells and whistles, they might have things you don't need and that you might find distracting.

For those of you who want to go even more 'old school,' write up that handwritten ledger and track your budget with pencil and paper. As long as you are consistent and diligent, it still works the same in the end!

Best Apps Out There for Expense Tracking

There is a long list of apps out there today that can help you track your expenses and, as a result, optimize your budget. These are some of the best we've seen that make all of the above more fun and more engaging. Keep in mind that new apps come out all the time, so keep an eye out for the latest and greatest, either through word of mouth or research on your own.

Digit

For many of us, the words 'fun' and 'savings' only work together when we don't have to think about the latter. Digit is an innovative app that links with your bank account. It then uses artificial intelligence to track and assess your spending, after which it calculates exactly what you can afford to put into savings. You literally do not need to do a thing after you set-up the account! Digit also offers an overdraft protection feature so that you can ensure it never puts all of your money into savings! Savings deposits average around 10-30 USD per week. Using Digit in tandem with your own scheduled deposits is a great way to increase savings slowly but surely... and without even having to think about it.

Clarity Money

The good news with Clarity Money is that you can access it via the internet on a desktop or laptop as well as via an app on your smartphone, making it a great choice for those of us who do not like to use smartphones as well as those of us who like options. Its app interface via smartphones is fun and engaging, delivering account activity updates and spending patterns in an easy-to-scan layout.

Clarity Money is especially good at staying on to of your spending in relation to the money you have coming in. One of its best features is its subscription tracker. How many times have you set up a subscription or a trial and then not realized that a new bill was coming due? With Clarity Money, you can stay on top of these pesky little bills. Additional benefits include automatic savings deposits and credit score tracking.

Wally

Wally is the king of the apps amongst the younger set, but it offers a range of benefits to any user. Wally's big advantage is its use of artificial intelligence to optimize your spending tracking. The AI interface gives you notes on your spending and advises you on what adjustments you should make to save more money.

This app does not link with banks; some may find this a disadvantage, but many feel relieved that they do not have to disclose sensitive financial information. One of its biggest advantages is the feature that allows you to share expenses with friends-- a perfect solution for group dinners, roommates, and more.

YNAB

YOU NEED A BUDGET... that's YNAB. This app takes your budget so seriously it makes your account for every single dollar in your bank. YNAB makes you assign "jobs" to every dollar so that it is allocated to anything from expenses to savings. You can use manual input if you want to limit your exposure to hacks, but YNAB also offers the option of automatic live linking with banks.

YNAB has an important goal with its budgeting program: to help you age your money. In other words, after using this app to streamline your budget, you will have money on hand from the month before instead of living paycheck to paycheck. YNAB also has a feature that allows you to free up money from one 'job' when you underspend to fund another area of spending. Fun and smart! YNAB often extends free trials so keep an eye out for these offers. Otherwise, it charges a very low monthly subscription fee of just $6.99 as of this writing.

Mvelopes

Remember our clever tip earlier in this chapter about keeping your spending cash in an envelope? This app is the digital version of that. Now imagine that! Mvelopes provides you with digital envelopes for different spending categories. You can use the money in each envelope until it's empty, helping you to stay aware of how much you have for each spending category and how quickly it is going out the door. An option such as Mvelopes is a great way to manage your spending before you spend it instead of scrambling to account for spending on miscellaneous expenses after the fact.

CHAPTER FOUR

Credit - It Isn't All Bad!

Credit is something that confuses almost everyone. The credit industry does send mixed signals, and it can be very difficult for the average consumer to get a handle on what is going on. Staying on top of your credit and learning to play the game well only takes a few tips, however. In no time at all, you can be on the road to a better score *and* enjoying the process.

Having good credit and playing the credit game well is an essential part of building good financial health. When you have credit on hand, too, it is a good way to help you save! You can use the credit constructively for larger purchases and use the extra funds to deepen your savings further.

That being said, let's take a look now at the basics of credit and what well-managed credit accounts can do for your financial well-being and savings.

Debt – Is it good for you???

Everyone has heard it or experienced it: creditors like you to be a little in debt. What you say? Why is that credit card company saying I don't have *enough* debt?? Why are they saying I don't have enough 'credit'? Isn't it good that I don't have credit cards and just use cash?

Well, no. There are many reasons for this, but one of the main ones is that banks and creditors can't track your behavior with cash spending. They can, however, with credit! What this means is that having some credit and using it wisely is the best way to demonstrate to lenders and creditors that you have a good handle on your financial affairs and know how to act responsibly.

In other words, having some debt and handling it responsibly is how credit card companies and lenders know you are a safe bet. The contradictions inherent in the credit system are frustrating for many, no doubt. But when you learn to play the game well, you can benefit hugely from it!

First Things First: What's Your Score?

You can't play the credit game well without knowing your score. The first thing you need to understand is that-- wait for it-- there is more than one score! That's right. Not only are there three different credit bureaus, there are also many different ways of calculating a credit score. For example, an auto lender might use one formula, while a mortgage company might use another!

Let's start out with the credit bureaus. You may know them. They are:

- Equifax
- Transunion
- Experian

These three bureaus receive reports from your creditors each month, then use that information to compile a score for you. This score is meant to be a reflection of your financial health and reliability. What does it take into consideration?

1. How many accounts you have open
2. The mix of accounts you have open
3. If you make payments every month and on time
4. How much of your credit you use
5. The length of your credit history

All of these factors are considered then packaged into a score that new lenders can use to determine your creditworthiness. The bureaus also offer as many as 25 different types of scores and parcel them out according to industry.

Paying Your Bills on Time

This is the easiest one to get right! Pay your bills every month and make sure you pay them on time. You can set up automatic payments with your creditor. As an alternative, if you bank online, you might also consider using your bank's automatic payment system to send out payments each month. Whichever approach you take, do it... and make sure you have budgeted the funds to cover all payments!

Getting the Mix Right

This one is a bit more nuanced and confusing for some. Lenders like to see a healthy mix on your credit report. This means they would like to see that you not only have credit cards but also have things like installment loans. An installment loan might be an auto loan or even a personal loan. They also like to see a good number of accounts! This is one of the credit factoids that throws the most people for a loop. That's right, they want to see that you have lots of accounts open! In fact, over 10 accounts are considered a good number of accounts to have open. One or two credit cards? Not gonna cut it, kid!

Personal loans are a good way to improve your credit. Again, this feels strange to many. Are you telling me that I have to go in debt to look good on paper to the credit bureaus? Well, yes, in part. Credit bureaus like to see an installment loan like a personal loan on your credit file. (Installment loans include auto loans, as an example.)

A big plus of personal loans is that you can use them to pay down credit card debt. It can work to your advantage in more ways; by consolidating your debt into one installment loan and then using that money to pay down your credit cards, chances are you can lower your total monthly payments while also giving a bump to your credit score.

Keep in mind that taking out a loan will momentarily ding your credit. Over time, however, making the payments on an installment loan like this can work wonders for your score and your financial health.

How Much Credit You Use-- Charge Small, Pay It All

In general, lenders do not want to see you using more than 30 percent of your available balance on your credit file. So, let's say you have five credit cards with a limit of 2000 USD each. This would total 10,000 in credit available to you. What they want to see is that you never charge more than 30 percent of that or 3000 USD. This shows them that you are using your credit constructively... and not using it to live beyond your means!

This is where a lot of people can actually have fun with credit and paying credit card bills. Make a game out of it! See how you can spread bills out across cards and then pay them off in full each month, making sure to never go above a total of 30 percent across your total credit file.

Pay a small household bill with a credit card each month then pay the whole amount off at the end of the card statement. Making regular payments and never missing one is, of course, one of the best ways to maintain or improve credit, as discussed, but *how* you pay matters, too! By charging a small amount that is less than 30 percent of your total credit card limit, you are showing the credit bureaus that you are not in "trouble" financially and spending too much... and you can have some fun with it along the way!

Using Credit Tracking Apps

There are a wide variety of credit tracking apps out there that you can use to stay on top of your credit. These can make credit fun for you, and they incorporate recommendations and offers that keep you engaged and help you improve your score. They are also a great way to keep an eagle's eye view of all your accounts.

Some popular options include:

- Mint
- Credit Karma
- Credit Sesame
- Nerd Wallet

The three bureaus also each offer their own apps that you can use to track your scores. There are a few things, however, you need to keep in mind when using third-party credit tracking apps such as Credit Karma or Nerd Wallet.

1. Their scores can be inflated
2. They are in the business of partnering you with new lenders

Now, with regards to inflated scores, this is done with two goals in mind: one, they want you to feel good about your score! And two, they want to entice you to take credit card or loan offers from their partners. They are not manufacturing these scores out of thin air, don't worry. For example, Credit Karma uses VantageScore to create your number-- this is not a fictional score, but it is not used by that many lenders and doesn't give you the most realistic picture of what lenders see when they look at your score. A VantageScore can be 50 points higher than the FICO score used by Capital One, for example.

So, take the good with the iffy! These apps are a great way to have fun with credit, monitor credit, and even accept new offers! You just want to make sure that you understand the realities of these trackers when using them.

A lot of these apps also have a fun option known as a credit estimator. This interface lets you make small adjustments to your credit file hypothetically and then see how these changes would adjust your score over time. Fun! But again, take it with a grain of salt. Your credit file is a living thing that is ever-evolving.

CHAPTER 5

When Emergencies Happen

It may well happen-- a time will come when you need extra cash on hand for an emergency situation. Whether it is a medical bill or a car repair, an event may occur that demands you dip into savings.

It's alright, don't fret! That's what your savings are there for. You just need to make sure that you have a game plan in place for getting those savings back and the right positive attitude to get you through a hard time.

Considering a Personal Loan

In chapter three we discussed the benefits a personal loan can bring with it. Not only do you get cash funds to help in an emergency, in this scenario, you may improve your credit by taking on a personal loan. Weigh your options: is the pending bill big enough to wipe out your savings? Would you be better off only using part of your savings then funding the rest with a loan?

Go through your monthly budget to make sure you can afford the monthly installments on a personal loan. If you, can and you can take the temporary ding to your credit, consider using a personal loan to help with the bills in an emergency, rather than wipe out your safety net of savings.

Dipping into Savings

As we discussed in the first chapter on savings basics, you want to maintain a core fund at all times in your savings. As mentioned, ideally this should be three months' worth of your living expenses. These are the last resort funds that you only use in case of job loss or serious emergencies

What if an extreme emergency occurs that is unrelated to job loss, such as a major hospital stay? Well, you just may need to dip into the reserve fund. After all of your hard work, you may see your savings take a ding.

However, you should never ever dip into your savings for anything other than a true emergency! What's not an emergency?

- An impulse buy
- An unnecessary material good (clothes, vehicles, etc.)
- A holiday
- A luxury item

There can sometimes be some wiggle room with clothes or vehicles. For example, if you need a car for work and your car breaks down or is totaled, that constitutes an emergency! If you are just buying a second car for weekend fun and games, that is not an emergency! Material and luxury items should only be purchased if and when you have the room in your cash flow and monthly budget for those purchases or if a loan to purchase one of those items is good for your credit at a given time.

So, let's say there is a true emergency. These might be:

- An unexpected injury
- A legal situation that requires representation
- A major car repair
- A hospital stay

It's okay! Go ahead and dip into the savings. That's what they were there for. Just make sure you do it with two things:

1. A plan!
2. A positive attitude!

The plan is easy because you've done it before! Sit down with your monthly budget and see how you can start building that savings reserve again. Maybe you will need to raise the stakes and increase the amount you save each month, even just temporarily. Plan out the year and for up to 5 years to come. Look at the big picture and see what you need to do to get back on top.

How to get a positive attitude? Here are a few tips to make that moment easier for you:

- Focus on your game plan for the future!
- Run through your savings program in your head
- Envision those funds piling up again
- Envision the safety and security you will once again have once they are back in place
- Focus on the good that dipping into your savings created! Maybe you helped a family member or saved your own life! The hard work you did saving that money created a lot of good in the world

for you and your family. Stay positive!
- Get excited to do it all again! You manifested your financial security once, and you can do it again.

CHAPTER 6

Having Fun with Savings: Games, Apps, Challenges & More

One of the best things about the modern age is all the financial apps out there. Not only have they given the average person access to investment and savings opportunities they might not have had access to in the past, but they have also made investing and saving fun! Plus, you can access your information anytime, anywhere via a smartphone, tablet, or laptop, giving you real-time data on your financial health and well-being.

Investment Opportunities

Once you have a savings buffer, you may want to consider investing some money. There are a number of fun options out there that give you hands-on experience with investing in new and inventive ways.

Peer-to-Peer Lending Investments

Investing in peer-to-peer lending is a great way to invest money while helping others find their own financial security. Peer-to-peer lending started gaining steam about a decade ago with companies such as Lending Club and Prosper. By bypassing the big banks, these companies are able to source funds from multiple individuals to facilitate loans. If you want to participate as a lender, you can see returns anywhere from 2 to over 5 percent annually. You can divide your investment between multiple loans, too, thereby limiting your exposure and risks.

Real Estate Crowdfunding Investment

Investing in real estate crowdfunding is another fun and innovative way to grow your money once you have a savings buffer in place. As with crowdfunded personal loans, real estate crowdfunding involves a number of separate individuals coming together to fund real estate projects and loans. Keep in mind that you may need to look into becoming an accredited investor in order to participate in some real estate crowdfunding enterprises. Others let you invest if they have a private mortgage REIT.

Microloans

Investing in microloans, like crowdfunding, is a good way to grow your money while helping others. Organizations such as Kiva, as an example, allow you to fund loans to small businesses and individuals in developing countries who might not have access to bank loans or meet the criteria for traditional loans.

Games and Challenges for Saving More

While you may not want to play games with money, there are games you can play when saving to make saving money more fun! These run the gamut from games to group challenges and are a way to stay engaged and invigorated by the process. Healthy competition with others, too, can up the stakes and ensure that you stay committed to your savings goals.

Treat Yourself Game

This game is just you against you! It is a good way to save and understand better how much you spend on miscellaneous luxury items.The game works like this-- when you want to make a luxury purchase, you have to deposit the same amount you spend on that purchase in your savings account! This works on two levels: it helps you pay attention to how much you spend on items that are not necessities of life, but also helps you save! It also has the virtue of making the experience of treating yourself that much more valuable since you are deepening your savings coffers in the process. How much can I afford to spend becomes how much I can afford to save... win-win for you!

Visualize!

A fun trick for engaging with your savings is using some visualization around what you will be able to do once you have savings in place. Try creating some mood boards if you are crafty that you can put up on your wall that visually manifest what your future will be like once you have reached your savings goals. Maybe you will own your own home for the first time, and maybe you will be able to buy that Mcqueen dress you always wanted, either way, use visual cues to create a mood board that manifests your financially secure future. Another great option— especially if you are not too crafty-- is to create a Pinterest board with some of your favorite things that you cannot afford right now. Share your Pinterest board with friends to level up on your excitement, and gather good ideas and feedback from your friends!

The Friendly Savings Challenge

The Friendly Savings Challenge involves you working in tandem with a group of friends. Set a timeline for your challenge-- maybe it's a month, maybe it's a year! You all want to see which of you can save the most in a specified period of time. You will have to be pretty transparent about your incomes since someone with a larger income might have an undue advantage. In these cases, a friendly handicap of that person in the challenge can help even things out and make the challenge fair. They might start at a deficit for the sake of the challenge, as an example. Competing against friends in this type of challenge is a great way to stay focused-- after all, we often care very much about looking bad in front of others, while we may not care as much if we fail ourselves!

No Spend Challenge

This is another group/friend challenge but works in the inverse of the savings challenge. Instead of seeing who can save the most, see which of you can spend the least! You can set rules that allow you to spend on the necessities of life (naturally!) but then make luxury or unnecessary purchases illegal in the world of the game. Which of you has the discipline to stick it out the longest? Which of you will get the greatest clarity on how much cash we waste on a regular basis and instead funnel those funds into deeper savings?

How Much Can I Trim?

This is a "you-against-you" challenge, and it is a competition you can sit down to each and every day. Go through your budget and see just how much excess fat there is. Do you really need that new pair of sneakers? What about new-to-you sneakers from a site such as Real Real instead of a brand new retail pair? Use this opportunity to really figure out where your excess cash is going and assess whether or not you are spending your cash in the best way possible.

CONCLUSION

We hope you have enjoyed learning about savings and exploring ideas around how savings can be a fun and positive experience for anyone. As you move forward on your savings journey, keep these things in mind.

Stay Positive!

No matter what happens-- be it an unexpected bill or the loss of a job-- you *will* get back on your feet! Maintain a positive attitude about your financial future and manifest the best of what is out there waiting for you. Setbacks don't mean that you have lost the war, only that you may have lost a battle or skirmish! Stay positive about your financial future and enjoy the experience of growing your savings.

Treat Yourself

Just as with a nutritional diet, so-called "cheat" days are what make your financial diet work. Every day and every month doesn't need to be about scrimping and saving. Treat yourself when you can and don't feel bad about it!

When you are dieting, it is actually beneficial to your diet to have a cheat day. This cheat day tells your body that you won't be starving it in the long term; as a result, it is less likely to store calories as fat as protection against future starvation. In a similar way, taking a break from your careful budgeting can give yourself a mental break. The rest and relaxation you have from treating you and yours to something makes it that much easier to stay on track.

Age your Money!

Get ahead of your bills and age your money. This gives you the security you need to feel better about your financial situation every day. Work toward the day when you will be using the money from last month's paychecks to pay the bills, instead of the money from this month's checks! Visualize what a relief it will be not to live paycheck to paycheck or have to go through a few weeks with only a handful of dollars in the bank.

Enjoy the Process!

Remember, saving money is about making a happier and healthier life for you and yours. Stay focused on the good that will come from having saved rather than focusing on penny-pinching! It is a fulfilling process that builds toward a better financial future, and an enjoyable one, too!

www.ingramcontent.com/pod-product-compliance
Lightning Source LLC
Chambersburg PA
CBHW071444170526
45158CB00005BA/1831

9 781090 814753